Burndown charts explained

Andrew Soswa

DEDICATION

To all of you, who continuously learn and improve your Agile delivery.

Carry on, my friends!

CONTENTS

ACKNOWLEDGMENTS

This book would not be possible without three of my friends
Supportive Bobby, resourceful Ram, and my mentor, Marcia.

1 INTRODUCTION TO AGILE CHARTS

Show me your burndown charts, and I will tell you how well your team performs – said the Coach.

This book is not for novice project leaders. If you are looking for an explanation to terms used in this book, go to the Scrum Guide, then come back to read this book. The book's purpose is to accelerate your learning and shorten your journey to Agile mastery. Each chapter will show you a chart, an explanation of the issue, and the most reasonable steps to fix it. But don't follow the information blindly. You should use this book as a building block to experiment with what you learned, practice it, and spread the knowledge further.

The burndown charts belong to an area of Agile project management reports. The charts assist the Scrum Master and the team to enhance operational effectiveness. During the Sprint, Scrum Master should use the diagram to observe and monitor the team's delivering every user story. After every iteration, the burndown chart should be analyzed and determined how the Agile team can improve during the next Sprint.

Calculating a burndown chart is a relatively simple exercise. There are a lot of online software tools that perform a pretty good job like Jira. For my spreadsheet, go to https://www.blueoceanworkshops.com to download it.

In this book, I will use the following project conventions:
- User stories are estimated on *adjusted* Fibonacci story's points
- The project's team consists of:
  - Scrum Master
  - Product Owner
  - 4 Team Member(s)
- In specific cases, other stakeholders are added for clarity
- Each Sprint (iteration) is two weeks long (10 working days)

2 HOCKEY STICK

It's your first implementation of Agile, and you just finished your first Sprint. You look at the Sprint Board and notice that all user stories are completed. Everyone feels proud and congratulatory notes are flying around... Until you hold a Sprint Delivery meeting and see a Completed yellow line sloping downwards on the last day. You think that this is probably not good.

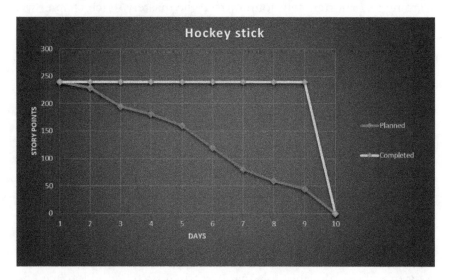

During Sprint Delivery, you sit down with the team and start discussing what happened and how to improve. If no one has ideas, you need to involve a professional Agile Coach to increase the team's **knowledge** about Agile methodology and help them develop mutual **trust** and **transparency**. If your firm does not allow trust, transparency, or knowledge sharing, your Agile adoption might be in trouble. Agile research indicates two outcomes for your team: disillusionment to Agile advantages or Agile hybridization to retain old management structures while try to receive benefits of Agile adoption.

Read other books on how to increase trust and transparency!

Retrospective # 1:

If your team members had many user stories and completed them but did not report them, then you have a coaching problem on your hands. Feedback:

You must have Daily Scrum (huddle or Standup) meetings throughout the Sprint. The purpose of Daily Scrum is to review the progress of each team member's work and share impediments that need to be resolved and hold oneself accountable to Sprint commitments. Without Daily Scrum, your charts will represent incorrect status.

Retrospective # 2:

The team is entrenched in old thinking (i.e., SDLC) to deliver outcomes at the last minute. Someone might ask Scrum Master, what is the due date of the deliverables? Isn't it at the end of the two-week Sprint?
Feedback:

It is essential to move the finished user story to Completed status. Don't wait until the last moment to move all done users stories into the Completed group. Avoid multitasking and work on one story at a time. Some Agile teams have a process to review the completed user story with the Product Owner during the Sprint and get it accepted before taking on the next user story.

Retrospective # 3:

The team claims that the user stories were completed when they were done. You check the user story points per user story and discover that all four of your team members had one user story in this Sprint (80, 40, 80, and 40). On the surface, all looks good.
Feedback:

You need to review your Backlog Refinement process with the Product Owner to ensure that there are no user stories that take more than approx. 20 hours. Although you might not estimate by time, the team has to understand that how long might each user story take in minutes and hours. User stories that are too big must be further broken into smaller user stories.

3 LINGERING EPICS

You just went through your first Sprint Delivery and Sprint Retrospective. You believe that the entire team understands Agile methodology, holds Daily Standups, and the rest of the project will be easy. You finish the next Sprint, and you notice the following chart. The user stories appear to be closed as they are completed, but what is that bump in the chart?

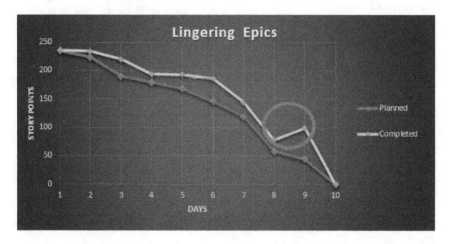

During Sprint Delivery, you review the Sprint's chart with your team and pinpoint to the mysterious jump. Yet, again on a surface, everything seems right; the team finished all user stories.

If you don't break your Epic user stories, you'll end up with a bigger problem – a team member completes 90% of the user story estimated at 80 story points. It is not done, so you cannot report it as Completed. Trust me, fixing this mess at the end is more challenging than properly refining and estimating in Backlog Refinement.

Retrospective:
The most likely cause was a user story with a lot of effort points that were just completed. For example, all user stories are estimated with 1, 3, 5, 8, or 13 points while there was one that has 40 points.

There are two possible reasons why it happened:

A. Epic user story

The team estimated user stories in the Backlog, and one of the user stories was an Epic. Product Owner prioritized the Epic to be worked in the next Sprint, and the team took it on.
Feedback:
Scrum Master (and the team) should immediately notice during Sprint Planning that the Product Owner wants to complete an Epic. Scrum Master must tell the Product Owner that the Epic is not adequately refined, might not be completed, or the Product Owner might not accept the end deliverable. Epics should be estimated differently

B. Unbreakable user story

Sometimes, a 40-points user story could not be further broken into smaller user stories.
Feedback:
From time to time, there is a user story that cannot be further refined and broken into smaller pieces. Scrum Master should:

a. Let the Product Owner know that the user story might not be completed on time. So a team member should work on it first.

b. Let Product Owner that the Product Owner might not accept deliverable because effort-heavy user stories usually contain a lot of specific tasks. The onus is on Product Owner to accept the responsibility

c. If more user stories are this big size, discuss with Product Owner to extend all Sprints, from now on into the future, by one week

4 OVER THE LIMIT

Your team is more confident that you can achieve more, or maybe it is management that desires more user stories completed. You say 'fine' and let the Product Owner push your team to take on more user stories that they have the capacity to achieve. You meet during Daily Scrum, you monitor the burndown chart daily, and it appears that they will not finish all their user stories. You provide this feedback to your team during Daily Scrum they sheepishly disagree. And boom, last day of Sprint comes, and during Sprint Delivery, you review the following chart.

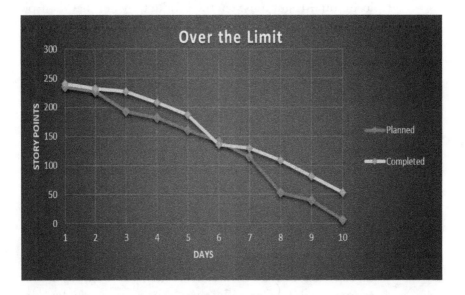

The Product Owner is furious because the product delivery plans need to be revised. With the Product Owner present, you muster all your courage and know that the conversation will not be easy.

Retrospective # 1:
If the team does not estimate user stories by time (see Appendix A), there are two Agile philosophies on loading user stories into the Sprint:

    A. Let the teamwork on their productivity from **the bottom up** where each team member will grow in skills and experience to refine, estimate, and complete a better deliverable

    B. Push user stories from **the top down** because each member must complete x amount of user story points. Sometimes Product Owner or Executive comes into Sprint Planning and bluntly states that 'These are stretch goals (or nice-to-haves), you'll do them if you have time in the Sprint.'

Feedback **on the bottom up:**
You can't allow your team to take more than they can complete. You need to know your team members' capacities and schedules.

Feedback **on the top down:**
Product Owner or your management dictate how much work they must do. Each member has to feel that they are working up to their capacity. You, and the Product Owner, and management must find other ways to increase your team performance.

Retrospective # 2:
You find out that you had a holiday, vacation, or suddenly someone got sick for a few days.

Feedback **on holidays or vacations:**
As a Scrum Master, you have to know when everyone on the team has holidays and vacations. If you are in France and your team is from India or Poland, they have different holiday and vacation policies.

Feedback **on sick time:**
If you have a competent and trustful team, no one should call in sick without a real emergency. If a person calls in sick, Scrum Master must:

    1. Provide support and ask if the member needs help

    2. Notify the Product Owner immediately. Maybe the user stories to be delivered by sick team members were on a Product Owner's critical path. Product Owner is not available or doesn't provide an answer, so you let the Sprint finish as planned.

5 REPRIORITIZED SPRINT

During the Sprint, one of the team members suddenly gets sick or quits. You immediately notify the Product Owner. After all, the user stories that this member was supposed to deliver are on a critical path. Unlike in the previous Sprint, the Product Owner takes action and replans what Sprint needs to deliver. You quickly meet with the team. User stories are added and removed; team members have user stories reassigned. You notice that your burndown chart has an unfamiliar vertical line.

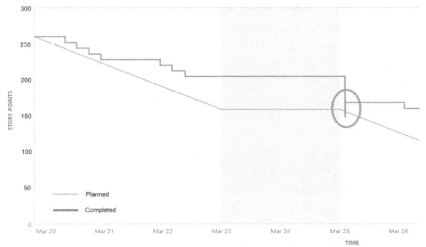

The above chart represents a real burndown chart from Jira.

Notice two factors in your reports:
- If you use Jira, the planned trendline does not change after Sprint is started. Jira should have a baseline and adjusted trendlines.
- If you create a burndown chart manually in Excel, the red vertical line will never appear on your chart. Only Jira can display it because Jira captures updates every minute.

Retrospective # 1:
Adding, removing, and reprioritizing user stories during a Sprint should not be taken lightly.
Feedback:
Since one of the Agile team's qualities is self-organizing, the team will frequently propose changes to their team, organization, and methodology's structure. Be careful not to be a 'Yes' man. As a Scrum Master, you are an 'architect' of the methodology and leader of the team. You should predict what happens if the team requests changes, and then you should explain to the team what effect these changes will have. Remember that if you do it once, you will **create a precedent,** and you will have to do it as often as the Product Owner or management requests.

Retrospective #2:
You have to be adept at knowing how to reprioritize within the Sprint.
Feedback:
Adding, removing, reprioritizing user stories during a Sprint should be done in an emergency only.

6 STRETCH GOALS

Your management must have many fancy terms for additional work. There are stretch goals, plan B, nice-to-haves, emergency fix (that truly is not), and lots of others. You and your team are working for your firm, and your management represents the best interest of the entire firm. Right?

Your management tells you what they told me, 'I don't care about Agile or project management; I only want results.'

You and the team feel under pressure to accept more work within the Sprint. As a Scrum Master, you are in no position to refuse.

Product Owner adds user stories to the Sprint and assigns them to people that the Product Owner feels should complete the work.

You review the chart during Sprint Delivery and start fearing for your position.

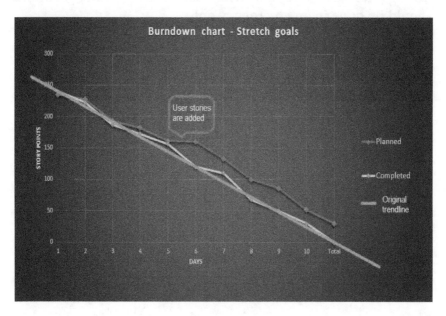

Retrospective:

The chart showed when user stories were added (day 5) and new blue Planned trendline from day six until the end. The team is overallocated, and you know that **the team will not be able to complete all their work.**

Feedback:

Except quitting on a spot, as a Scrum Master, you should:

A. When user stories are added, meet with the Product Owner to:
   a. Notify that without adding time or additional team member, your current team will not complete all user stories
   b. Find out the priority of the added user stories.
   c. Reprioritize your Sprint only if you absolutely must – otherwise, leave it all as is (plan to fail)
B. During Sprint Delivery describe why the team was not able to deliver all user stories and provide this feedback to Product Owner and management

7 WORKING OVERTIME

So you and your team agreed to work longer hours in this Sprint. You know that Agile seeks balance to create continuous and sustainable working hours. You can probably pull 80 hours per week once, but then, if your team trusts you, they will start going through five stages of grieving on your project. When they reach the fifth stage, you will have a team that is burned out or no team at all because they would all leave your firm.

You should also know the answer if you and your team are salaried or hourly workers? In my experience, salary workers are asked to work longer hours because they are not hourly. Additionally, the management expects that a salaried worker works until the work is done.

As a result, you display the following chart to the Product Owner and the management.

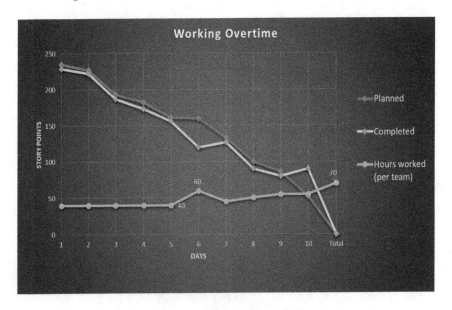

Retrospective:

In your detailed written report, you provide your feedback on what happened and how you solved it. Don't forget to add the word **'unsustainable working hours'** when displaying the diagram with extra hours spent by your team.

Feedback:

In your detailed written report, you provide your feedback on what happened and how you solved it. Don't forget to correctly display longer hours worked by your team to deliver all deliverables:

- Five members fully allocated per day equals to 40 hours
- On day 6, the team spent additional time to discuss the changes
- On day 10, the team spent 70 hrs to complete all work.

8 EARLY FINISH

The team works hard and delivers all their user stories early. Now, is that a problem?

It depends who overviews the chart.

- The management would claim that the team members are not taking enough work in the Sprint.
- The Product Owner would claim that the user stories are overestimated with effort points.
- Team members claim that they were able to finish early due to greater team collaboration and creating small efficiencies

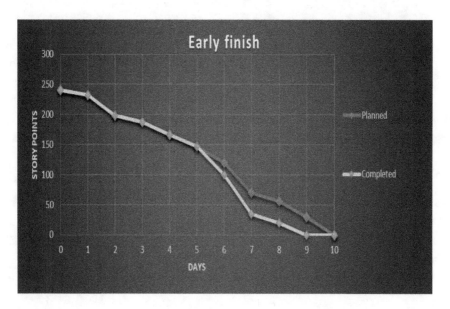

Retrospective #1:
If you pass an unrefined message from the management to the team, your team most likely feels underappreciated. The team might feel bad by being called slackers (not taking enough user stories to work on) or, worse, liars (overestimation). You must display tact and political acumen while dealing while communicating messages between your team and the management.
Feedback:
First, explain to the management and Product Owner why the team was able to finish early. Second, note the steps that you are taking to ensure that the problem will not occur in the future.

Retrospective # 2:
Usually, the burndown chart will show that team completes their user stories early on the last day. However, as a great Scrum Master, you have to design a tracking spreadsheet that will show you how much work is still in individuals' workstreams in the Sprint.
Feedback:
Create a per-member burndown chart. For some, it might be a bit of too much administrative overhead; however, for your additional 15 minutes, you will be able to verify who is the top performer and who slacks off. You must **trust but verify** their transparency and teamwork.

9 SME CHART

Agile methodology recommends and strives to create sustainable work for a team composed of the same team members over the length of the project. The team's consistency allows us to process-ize non-productive time (all Sprint events) and develop Objective and Key Results (OKR) improvements.

What happens when your team is composed of Subject Matter Experts (SMEs)? How would your burndown chart appear?

There are two recommended approaches:
1. If you have a consistent team and a few SMEs, then:
   a. Create Sprints for your team
   b. Create separate Sprints for your SMEs
2. If you have only SMEs, then do not divide them into teams and create Sprints as if they were one team. Create one **SME chart** per Sprint for all SMEs.

In approach # 1, you will still receive benefits of tracking and improving performance for your team and the SMEs. The separation of the team from SMEs appears as not such a big issue until you start collecting data for your Velocity charts (see my next book, *Velocity charts explained* coming soon).

In the approach #2, the SME burndown chart will allow you to keep track of the work within the Sprint. Reviewing the **SME chart** after the Sprint finishes are pointless; SMEs' work is delivered. You will not be able to improve future Sprints. On the other hand, what you must do is to **keep track of the SME completing their tasks within the Sprint**.

Retrospective:

Unchecked tasks tend to expand the timeline.

While Agile proscribes self-organization and transparency, you need to **trust but verify**. If you do not have Daily Standup with your SMEs, they will most likely deliver on the last day of the Sprint.

Here is a concrete example of a task to be completed by one SME:

1. SME is available on Wednesday (day 3 of the Sprint) for 8 hours and Tuesday (day 7 of the Sprint) for 4 hours
2. SME estimated that to complete the task will take 10 hours

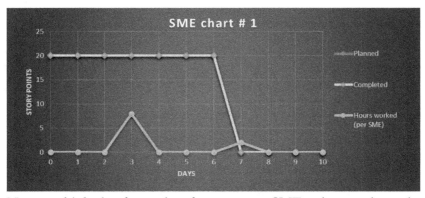

Now, multiply the above chart by two more SMEs where each one has only one task in the Sprint and is allocated on a different day. In SME chart # 2, you will notice that the burndown chart does not make much sense, and only daily check-in with your SMEs will ensure that their tasks are completed on time.

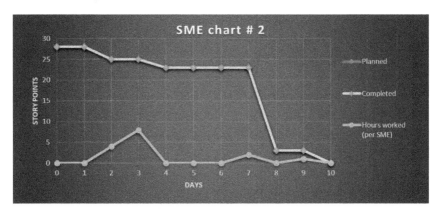

10 WATERFALL RELEASE

Businesses desire to implement Agile methodologies because they want to benefit from early product delivery to the customer. If you have been in the Agile project management field for a while at various firms, you must have completed at least one Agile Transformation project. Now, you know that trying to fit Agile processes without company-wide transformation is pointless. Some firms decide to retain all their forms and try to force the Agile product's delivery model. For example, in top-down hierarchical firms, when an Executive dictates what needs to be done, the team has to drop Agile methodology, complete the Executive's request, and then go back to working in Agile fashion. It simply does not work like that, and your Agile Transformation is in the name only.

Some firms, however, after careful planning, can create their unique wagile or agilefall techniques where they can merge waterfall and Agile methodologies. **The success of hybrid implementations is based on management's adaptability and appetite to experiment and innovate**. The firm has to accept that part of the work will be scrap until a superior process emerges. I have heard multiple times that how innovative a firm is, but management wants 100% error-free delivery. As a result, there is no room for innovation.

Still, I want to congratulate some of you who were able to design a successful hybrid methodology. In my experience, the following will happen:
- The entire team will consist of full-time members, SMEs, and vendors
- You will most likely use Jira Scrum template
- The Sprints will vary in length between 3 weeks to 2-months
- The Sprint deliverables will be based on a production-ready product release to the end-user. Some Scrum Masters call it Release Train or Release Sprint. It looks more like a mini-project.

Retrospective:

Since you are going to have various groups present in one burndown chart, you need to determine how each group or person will provide updates on completed work. My recommendation is:

Vendors report by milestone with a bi-weekly check-in on % of completed work

Each full-time team member reports during Daily Standup

SMEs report bi-weekly or are asked to attend Daily Standup

Additionally, **in the waterfall/agile hybrid, request that internal team members estimate their work by time (not by effort)**. Reporting by hours burned allows:

adjusting the time allocation of each team member when they are not fully allocated to the project

congruent visual report with how SMEs and vendors report (by hours burned)

The resulting chart can be visually very messy; you might want to divide it into separate charts for SMEs, vendors, and internal teams. Do whatever you need to make you effective in responding to change every day.

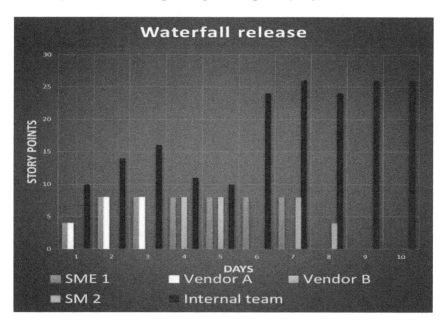

ABOUT THE AUTHOR

Andrew Soswa is an accomplished coach and trainer with over 20 years in leadership and project management roles. His passion is to help others develop leadership and organizational skills. Connect with him via his personal website https://andrewsoswa.website

Notes:

Appendix A – Estimating by effort & hours

Before Backlog Refinement:

1. Scrum Master understands team allocation and member's capacity
   a. Determines time allocation to the project per member (i.e., member A – 40 hrs/week, member B – 20 hrs/week)
   b. Calculates time spent on project's deliverables vs. management time

$$AC - ET = PC$$

   AT - Allocated capacity
   ET - Add time spent on Sprint events (2 hrs Sprint Planning, 6 hrs Backlog Refinement, 1 hr Sprint Delivery, 4 hrs demo, .5 hrs Sprint Retrospective, 2.5 hrs Daily Scrum + 1 hr non-productive time= 17 hrs)
   PC – Productive capacity
   Note: for fully (40 hrs/week) allocated team member, on 2-week Sprints, the PC is between 60 to 65 hrs

2. PO prioritize user stories to be refined (before Backlog Refinement starts)

During Backlog Refinement:

3. Team refines user stories to get DOD with PO guidance
4. Immediately after refining a story, the team begins estimating
5. The result of Backlog Refinement is set of (a) prioritized (b) refined (c) estimated user stories

Before Sprint Planning:

6. PO prioritizes user stories according to the project's needs

During Sprint Planning:

7. Each team member takes a set of user stories (only those from Backlog that are refined, estimated, and prioritized)
8. Each team member estimates their own user stories by minutes and hours that it takes to complete each user story.
   a. If a member adds all hours and is below Productive Capacity, member adds for more user stories
   b. If a member is over PC, then a member gives a user story back to Backlog and trade back for a smaller user story
   c. All is good if member estimates the sum of all user stories at his/her Productive Capacity
9. When everyone is at capacity, Sprint Planning is over, and work starts.

Appendix B – Estimating Epics

If you first create Epics and then break them into user stories, then you are in luck. This guide applies to you.

The purpose of creating Epics is to create a high-level structure of the project, estimate them, and create a feasible timeline of the project. You know that you cannot refine and estimate all user stories. Sometimes, the Product Owner does not know them all upfront; other times, the user stories change so drastically based on end-user feedback that it is a futile exercise.

Here are the steps:
Before Epics Refinement:
1. Product Owner (or a team) creates a roadmap that consists of Epics that need to be completed to develop MVP of the product
2. Product Owner chooses a non-numeric scale
   a. Shirt sizes; Small, Medium, Large, and X-Large
   b. Colors; red, orange, yellow, green, blue, indigo and violet
During Epics Refinement:
3. Each Epic is analyzed and refined to a point where team members can start estimating its size
   a. If necessary, Epics are further broken into smaller Epics
4. Dependencies between Epics are discussed
5. After refining an Epic, the team estimates the Epic with a non-numeric scale
After Epics Refinement:
6. Product Owner inserts the results into the roadmap and starts tracking and reporting the progress

www.ingramcontent.com/pod-product-compliance
Lightning Source LLC
LaVergne TN
LVHW022127060326
832903LV00063B/4806